[handwritten: Lots of Love from Abigail xx]

THE EPITOME OF STRENGTH

"LET ME ENCOURAGE YOU AS YOU ENCOURAGE YOURSELF"

ABIGAIL OHEMAA AFRIYIE

JLG Publishing

Copyright © 2018 by Abigail Ohemaa Afriyie

THE EPITOME OF STRENGTH

ISBN 978-0-9956641-2-8

Published and Formatted by JLG Publishing

www.jlgpublishing.weebly.com

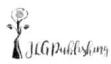

THE EPITOME OF STRENGTH

CONTENTS

ACKNOWLEDGMENTS

~

I WANT TO THANK THE ALMIGHTY FATHER for giving me the heart to start talking about his word; without him I am nothing. Through it all, I learnt to trust and depend on the Lord, even the days where I wanted to give up, God had a way of showing me it wasn't about me but about his people. God, I am grateful.

There are several delightful people who contributed in uncountable ways to my experiences in writing this book…

MY SUGARPLUM, MY CONFIDANT, MY HUSBAND KOFI; day by day together our love grows into a bond that God continues to watch over. When I was weak, you pick me up and made sure I was first. You are the most selfless person I know, and I can't wait to keep unfolding more days, weeks and years with you. I love you.

YAA BONO, MY MOTHER; you didn't come to the UK in vain, I will make sure of that. I love you so much.

Ralph Boakye-Mensah; through the ups & downs, you will always be my dad. Love Always.

Mr John Kingsley Mensah & Mrs Margaret Mensah; I thank God for your life. You are the best In-laws a girl can have, thank you for your prayers, support and your love. I appreciate it from the bottom of my heart. May God continue to strengthen you both. I love you both very much.

Abrafi; the first child that made me a sibling, through it all, and I mean through it all, you have kept me grounded. Keep pushing, your breakthrough is around the corner. Love you Sis.

To my Godsons Noah and Nathaniel; never let anyone discourage you or distract you from your purpose. You will both be great. I love you both.

My pastor, my Lady Reverend Anna Vanderpuye; God really blessed me with a Pastor that has a heart big enough for everyone. God knows I am so grateful for your life. Thank you for being you.

Vicky Osei; from day one, you have been pushing me, directing me, encouraging me. Thank you for being the big cousin I could look up to.

Karina Etienne; the challenges we have faced together is a book within itself, but God has allowed us to flourish and I am humbled that you are by my side. Karina, I love you.

Lucy Ahatty; one of my annoying but loveable Sisters. I mean we go way back, I know you always have my back and God knows I am grateful for your life. More Grace Sis.

Aunty Lahadi; thank you. Your experiences and your heart have shaped me to be the person I am today. May God continue bless you.

ZINA MAHAMA; thank you for your enthusiasm, your support and your love and most importantly my Godson Noah. I love you both with all my heart.

RICHARD ANNOR; the big brother I never had. Thank you for being you. You're an amazing father and may God continue to bless you.

EDITH WIREDU; a friendship that blossomed into a sisterhood, girl it was meant to be, they won't understand, it doesn't matter, God holds us together.

DANIEL GONZALEZ my Spanish Brother; Bro God has big plans for you. The love you show me & my family will never be forgotten. Mibanga Bespoke it's coming.

JENICA LEAH; we met and never separated. You believed even when it seemed impossible to. You are an inspiration and you never stopped looking out for me. In fact, you are the inspiration behind the name of this book. God bless you.

AMA OWUSU-DWUBENG, BRIDGET ADDAI, LESSANDRA FALOLU; you have seen me at my best and have seen me at my worst. If the world had more women of you around, it would surely be a better place. God bless you abundantly, individually you have made an impact in my life and I am grateful.

LADIES IN WAITING TEAM - PHILIPA BROBBEY, LUCY DADSON AND SENA WORGORMEBU; may God bless you and elevate each one of you. May your obedience and sacrifice never be in vain.

MY GRATITUDE TO MY FAMILY WORLDWIDE, who have been by side through thick and thin. Your encouragement, your principles and your prayers have kept me pushing.

I CANNOT FORGET THOSE WHO I ENCOUNTER DAILY or those who I have only met once that have had an impact on my life. Thank you. I appreciate you and may God remember you in your prayers.

FOREWORD BY EMMANUEL SMITH

∼

We unfortunately live in a world where looking good has become such an obsession that people would rather keep the reality of their struggles a secret from even their loved ones. I have personally read a few books in my time but this book by this amazing woman of God breaks down scriptures and relates them to practical life. She gives examples in the book on experiences that a lot of people including myself can relate to and not just that but with scriptures that can be used in a time of prayer so that we can effectively overcome most of the daily issues we face in our everyday lives. I therefore implore you to read this book with an open heart and great expectation that your life will be greatly impacted by the time you finish reading this amazing book.

FOREWORD BY ERIC REVERENCE

~

The Epitome of Strength is an outstanding book for everyday life and one which is so relevant to today's society needs. After reading the book, I was truly inspired and impacted with a genuine sense of hope that I can overcome every obstacle. The scriptures and poems gives the reader many tools of how to deal with situations in life and brings about hope and restoration. A well written, simple but powerful book that will help and transform many lives in today's society. I will highly recommend this book and a massive applaud to the author, Ohemaa Afriyie Mensah on this masterclass.

OPENING PRAYER

"I pray that this book will bless you in every aspect of your life. May the prayers and poems be a blessing in your life and those around you. Continue this journey of life with faith and you shall surely make it.

Wake up early and start the day with God. Putting God in your day makes a difference. Enrich yourself with knowledge and understanding.

Be strong and endure.

Love and honour yourself.

May the blessing of God be upon you."

- Abigail Ohemaa Afriyie

In loving memory of my Uncle Kwaku Nyamekye.
I regret not telling you that I was writing this book as I thought that we
would speak again, but I know you are not in pain anymore and you are in a
place where we are all aiming to be.
May your soul rest in perfect peace, I will forever love you.

To my Grandmother Ama Pokuaa.
There is not a day that goes by that I don't miss you.
You will never be forgotten.

SCRIPTURES TO GET YOU THROUGH DIFFICULT TIMES.

"Be strong in the Lord and in his mighty power. Put on the full Armor of God, so that you can take your stand against the devil's schemes."
- Ephesians 6:10-11

1 CORINTHIANS 10:13

The temptations in your life are no different from what others experience. And God is faithful. He will not allow the temptation to be more than you can stand. When you are tempted, he will show you a way out so that you can endure.

In difficult situations, we do question God and for a split second we forget that he has written our stories already so why question him? God hasn't forgotten you, trust me I know. This is just a gentle reminder to let you know you are a strong soldier and you can bear the difficulty and pain you're going through; because God wouldn't give you something you wouldn't be able to handle. Remember, you are blessed and highly favoured.

PSALM 23:4

Even when I walk
through the darkest valley,
I will not be afraid,
for you are close beside me.
Your rod and your staff
protect and comfort me

You may reach a stage in your life where things may come to a stand-still, or a place where wickedness is happening. You may reach a stage where no matter how many people surround you, you still feel alone. You may even be faced with a situation that is rising and you cannot seem to find a way out. The place you are in can be so dark and weary that you don't even know if there will be light. No matter how dark and deep the path is that you are walking on now, you will never be alone; for God will comfort you through this stage. He will protect and guide you. Fear not, for God will always walk with you no matter the place or situation. Hold on and do not give up on God.

PROVERBS 12:25

Worry weighs a person down;
an encouraging word cheers a person up.

Anxiety is a cause of worry yet most of us don't even realise it. Decision making can put us in an awkward place and cause us to over-think about things without even noticing. All it takes is an encouraging word to put us back on track and help us get through these stages of anxiety. My word for you today is take your time – all is well. That decision you must make, don't do it alone, lean on God's understanding no matter if you think you can vision the road ahead. Allow him to direct your path and you will reach that goal all in good time. Stay blessed.

ECCLESIASTES 3:1

For everything there is a season,
a time for every activity under heaven.

There is a time for Everything. Yes, indeed it is very true. Most people will agree with this scripture but deep down there is doubt within themselves; we have all been there including myself. To truly understand this scripture, we must understand that God will always make a way no matter what. Certain pressures come from humans, especially when certain questions come up;

"When will you get married?"
"When are you having a baby?"
"When will you find a better job?"

We must know within ourselves that God's timing is the best time. So, when these questions are asked, give them the word confidently and say;

"There is a time for everything."

My prayer is that whatever your heart desires, God will surprise you in a way you won't expect. Do not look at your current situation and doubt God. Hold on and allow him to work within you, for your time is coming, stand boldly and know that God will fight for you. Be blessed.

PSALM 119:25

I lie in the dust;
revive me by your word

Everyday can be a constant battle that you may be having with your-self and things around you. Distractions no matter where you turn as you keep trying to make it through the day. A spirit of heaviness falls upon you and you feel like you are in chains emotionally. Just cry out and allow God to revive you. It is hard to hear God when you allow everything around you to block you from him. God will breathe life unto you day by day, so that your spirit will be whole and that your soul made right. May you find comfort in God's word and allow it to make you pure. Be blessed.

Recommended song: 'Breathe into me oh Lord' by Fred Hammond.

1 CHRONICLES 16:34

*Give thanks to the L*ORD*, for he is good!*
His faithful love endures forever.

We acknowledge God and give thanks. No matter what you go through in life, one thing that is permanent is that God's love endures forever. Always give thanks to the Lord for where he has brought you. Discover within yourself a heart of thanksgiving because there is a reason why you are still here. Allow for God to reign within you and know that there is no love greater than God's love.

JAMES 1:2-3

²Dear brothers and sisters,[a] when troubles of any kind come your way, consider it an opportunity for great joy. ³ For you know that when your faith is tested, your endurance has a chance to grow.

There was a time when if I saw this scripture I would read it once over and turn away. Why? Because I didn't understand that any trouble that came my way would build me up. When you go through stormy challenges, it can cloud your vision for what is ahead of you. I can now tell you from experience, when your faith is tested and you go through the battles and the pain, you become a source of strength for yourself and others.

Battles will come and go but I pray that you find that endurance within yourself, so you may grow and flourish.

ISAIAH 41:10

Don't be afraid, for I am with you.
Don't be discouraged, for I am your God.
I will strengthen you and help you.
I will hold you up with my victorious right hand

Most of us face battles that others are not aware of and at times it can become a dark road. When I read and think of this scripture particularly it gives me courage to know that no matter what I am faced with, God is upholding me with his right hand. Allow God to strengthen you to face those battles and no matter what the world may tell you, God is telling you through his word 'do not be afraid and do not be discouraged for I am with you.' Don't give up. God has you.

HEBREWS 11:1

Faith shows the reality of what we hope for; it is the evidence of things we cannot see.

Do you believe that having faith can shift so many things in your life? I certainly do. I'm not talking about small faith with a bit of doubt but unshakable faith which allows you to know whatever God has for your life, it will surely come to pass. No matter what the doctor's report will say, no matter what people around you are saying, or even if the situations looks bleak. Having faith in God and knowing that his will, will be done in your life alone can turn things around for you. Have more faith and watch things turn around for your good.

EPHESIANS 6:10

A final word: Be strong in the Lord and in his mighty power.

Pray early for God to give you strength for whatever the day, week, or month may bring. When you have problems, or get into certain situations, go to the throne and not your phone. I am encouraging you that whatever it is, you can do it. Weakness does not live in you anymore. May you be strong in the Lord and find power in the word of God.

PSALM 34:18

The L{ORD} is close to the broken-hearted;
he rescues those whose spirits are crushed.

Have you ever felt broken before?

Where only your tears can speak for how you feel and no amount of words can help you through the next ten minutes, or even the next hour, day or week. Brokenness is an empty feeling which can swerve a person into different directions. There is only one thing I know and one thing I can say to anyone who is experiencing this feeling; the Lord is near you. You may not feel it right now, especially how the situation is going or how it went. It may feel like he is distant but when you are ready to acknowledge him, he is and will always be by your side, for he rescues the crushed in Spirit.

3 JOHN 1:2

Dear friend, I hope all is well with you and that you are as healthy in body as you are strong in spirit.

This scripture is self-explanatory and is a scripture everyone should be able to stand on. In life, you never know when your health can be threatened and dealing with it can be another thing. My prayer for you is that your health is well in Jesus name. Speak it into your life. The doctors may have a report but God has the final say. No matter how challenging the situation may be at hand, you are well in Jesus name. Be covered under the blood of Jesus and let the word of God speak for you. You are well and you shall do well.

ROMANS 5:4

And endurance develops strength of character, and
character strengthens our confident hope of salvation.

When we go through things in life, no matter how bad it may seem, how hard it may be or how long it lasts, we must know that there is a light at the end of every tunnel. Endurance is the ability to bear an unpleasant or difficult process or situation, without giving way. I strongly believe that God doesn't give us more than we can handle. Being able to endure a situation builds our inner man. It develops our character and makes us the person we are today. Developing endurance finds a way for us to be able to build our confidence in God, and know that he will strengthen us at any given point within the situation. I pray that you will not allow your situation to overtake you and that your inner man be strengthened. Look only unto God for the salvation of hope, for your confidence lies within.

PSALMS 3:3

But you, O Lord, are a shield around me;
you are my glory, the one who holds my head high.

God tenderly lifts our heads, looks in our eyes, exalts us and lets us know we are not alone in our time of sadness. It is only God who can lift our head during pain and grief. When looking at this psalm it describes how David fled from his son Absalom and he was alone amid nowhere. King David knew all about shame and pain. He knew what it was to be depressed and overwhelmed. He understood sadness and grief. King David also knew what it was like to have God take him by the chin, lift his head and offer hope. My prayer is that no matter what you are facing today, God does have a plan to see you through. Don't give up; it is a part of your story. God will use you in a mighty way, a way that will be indescribable. God Is faithful to show you fresh new perspectives and life lessons through any grief experience you face. It is only God's comfort that can heal you. Look to him only.

SCRIPTURES TO ENCOURAGE FAITH AND BELIEF.

"*B*ut without faith it is impossible to please Him, for he who comes to God must believe that He is, and that He is a rewarder of those who diligently seek Him."

- Hebrews 11:6

DEUTERONOMY 5:33

Stay on the path that the Lord your God has commanded
you to follow. Then you will live long and prosperous
lives in the land you are about to enter and occupy.

The testing times have begun and this is when our faith gets tested as well. Believe it or not, this is when your breakthrough is on its way. Do not allow anything to hinder your blessings. Even your nearest and dearest may distract you but be still and allow yourself to hear from God in these testing times. Walk in obedience for you will prosper.

PSALM 71:3

Be my rock of safety
* where I can always hide.*
Give the order to save me,
* for you are my rock and my fortress.*

When everything around you does not seem to be going to plan and you feel as if you have no one to turn to. When you are surrounded by people but you feel alone. When there is no foundation stable. Christ the rock of salvation will be the rock you shall stand. Go to him, for there is refuge in time of tribulation. Yes, speak to him for he will listen.

PHILIPPIANS 4:19

*And this same God who takes care of me will supply all
your needs from his glorious riches, which have been
given to us in Christ Jesus.*

When we pray, we find it easier to speak about the problems we are
going through and pray that God will answer them.

Attention! Our God is a prayer answering God. He will supply all
your needs according to his riches in Jesus Christ. So, next time when
you pray, thank him for that miracle you will receive. Thank him for
favour you will receive within your business. Thank him for the
health of that family member who has not been well. All shall be well
with you.

EZEKIEL 36:26

And I will give you a new heart, and I will put a new spirit in you. I will take out your stony, stubborn heart and give you a tender, responsive heart.

Change is something that challenges us every day. Growth is what we desire in different aspects of our lives. It doesn't take a human to do that because the task is so big and it will only be temporary. Every day is a learning curve. Let us stop chasing our old selves which doesn't bring us any peace and let us allow God to change our hearts, so that we may grow.

ACTS 10:34

Then Peter replied, "I see very clearly that God shows no favouritism.

God shows no favouritism. When reading Acts chapter 10, it talks about Cornelius the Gentile who feared God and who was prayerful. In those times, the Gentiles were not seen to be people who were respected and most would say they were like pagans. Peter who was a Jew disregarded the fact that a Jewish man could associate or befriend a Gentile. It was not until Cornelius had a visitation and recited it to Peter, that Peter realised God shows no favouritism and loves those who fear him and does what is right. At times, we are as guilty as Peter without us even knowing and we act different towards different tribes, races, nations and situations, etc. Let us remember that we are one and being prejudice does not allow us to be fruitful. Every day is a learning curve, let us learn to love one another better each day.

2 THESSALONIANS 3:16

Now may always the Lord of peace himself give you his peace and in every situation. The Lord be with you all.

No matter what Job you have, no matter what car you drive, no matter if you are married, no matter what your situation; it will not guarantee you peace. Having peace is something that you cannot buy. It is a huge blessing to have peace around you and most importantly in your heart. May the Good Lord grant peace within your home and within any situation you are going through. David who had trouble around him was granted peace by God. I challenge you to give your heart to God first and I tell you peace will follow you abundantly.

PHILIPPIANS 4:13

***For I can do everything through Christ, who gives me
strength.***

A very famous scripture which I see around all the time, yet I never
had a full understanding of it until now. It took me a while to accept
this scripture as I felt people I knew in my past used this scripture
without no meaning. They would flamboyantly say it without understanding so I would hide myself from the scripture.

Until God started placing this scripture on my heart and the more
I tried to hide from it, the more it kept coming back. I then realised in
my quiet time that I kept associating the scripture with the people I
despised from my past, instead of realising it was God's word and I
should have been receiving and associating this scripture with him
and no one else.

It is a powerful scripture and you must receive it with faith.

If Christ doesn't strengthen you, you can fall short; no matter if
you think you're the best in your talents and your gifts in life. Believe
it and pray it back to God and may you exalt in greatness; because you
can do ALL things through Christ who will continue to strengthen
you.

PROVERBS 10:22

*The blessing of the L*ORD *makes a person rich,*
and he adds no sorrow with it.

To be blessed is not about getting rich. To be blessed is not about assets or what you may gain from material things. When you are truly blessed by the Lord, you are blessed with affluence and victory. Just as the Lord commanded for Abraham to leave everything behind and follow him to a new land, Abraham and his descendants until today are still blessed. It is only God that blesses; not man. I promise you if you labour in being blessed by the Lord, sorrow will never be your portion. If you believe it, claim it and receive it. Labour and be blessed.

MATTHEW 6:31-33

31 "So don't worry about these things, saying, 'What will we eat? What will we drink? What will we wear?' 32 These things dominate the thoughts of unbelievers, but your heavenly Father already knows all your needs. 33 Seek the Kingdom of God[a] above all else, and live righteously, and he will give you everything you need.

Seek ye first the Kingdom of God and his righteousness and all things shall be added unto you. A very popular verse in the book of Matthew, in fact it was also a popular hymn which I sang in primary school. It is not until I went to a convention with my Bishop Dag Heward-Mills that I got a clear understanding of this verse.

You see you cannot fully understand verse 33 without reading verse 31 and 32. Verse 31 talks about our worries over little things and verse 32 talks about our Heavenly Father knowing our needs. Verse 33 then explains to us what we should do.

Believe it or not, as humans we worry way too much about the little things and as a believer in Christ, we should know that fear is not of God. Fear and worry are cousins and we should not harbour them at all. I guarantee if you make a covenant to seek the kingdom of God, he will supply your needs and more. Be about your Father's kingdom and you will NEVER be last.

HEBREWS 11:6

And it is impossible to please God without faith. Anyone who wants to come to him must believe that God exists and that he rewards those who sincerely seek him.

To please God without faith is surely impossible.

There are so many examples I can give but one always springs to mind and it will be Abraham and his faith in God. Because of his faith, God loved Abraham so much despite his wrongdoings and he was counted as one of the most righteous. You must get to a place in your life where you yearn to develop the spirit of faith. Do not listen to those who question your faith and do not believe, for they are people who don't believe in God but want blessings.

May the Spirit of faith be your portion. May you grow and develop faith like Abraham who did not look at his present situation but trusted and believed that God would bless Sarah with the fruit of the womb. May your faith in God grow and may he reward you as you sincerely seek him. Your faith will move mountains. May you be blessed and have that unshakeable faith.

JOSHUA 24:15

But if you refuse to serve the Lord, then choose today whom you will serve. Would you prefer the gods your ancestors served beyond the Euphrates? Or will it be the gods of the Amorites in whose land you now live? But as for me and my family, we will serve the Lord.

This powerful scripture came up at a Sunday service at church and it had me in my thoughts.

I started losing friends when I started to serve the Lord more. It was sad at first but it opened my eyes and showed me what I had to do to look forward. As you serve God, you may look foolish in the eyes of others but continue to serve him as your work will never be in vain. Look at the life of Noah, everyone thought he was foolish to build an ark but when the right time came, the same people were begging to get on that 'foolish' ark.

No one said it would be easy to serve God but I am telling you that there is a difference between those who serve God genuinely and whole heartedly, and those who do not. Choose God and he will bless you abundantly

PROVERBS 3:7

Don't be impressed with your own wisdom.
Instead, fear the LORD and turn away from evil.

Do not rely on your own wisdom… How many times has it got you into trouble?

Plenty of times right, which can often lead to heartache. Trust me I have been there. True wisdom comes from God and it is important to seek his face before embarking on any important decisions, or path you choose to take. Wisdom is a principal thing, therefore get wisdom.

Seek wisdom from above so that it may guide and govern your life. May Godly wisdom be your portion. Be blessed.

ISAIAH 60:22

The smallest family will become a thousand people,
and the tiniest group will become a mighty nation.
At the right time, I, the Lord, will make it happen.

Our God works in mysterious ways and sometimes, or should I say most times, I sit down and reflect on the path that I have been on and the path he will lead me on. God's time is the best time, even when we don't realise it. Things you have prayed on for such a long time, when it eventually comes unexpectedly, we don't know how to receive it. Or sometimes we are in a rush for things and we may think we are ready, but God is the one who knows best.

May the Grace of God locate you and give you a heart of patience. May you receive faith and know that God will move you forward in life. Believe it and receive it.

1 TIMOTHY 1:7

They want to be known as teachers of the law of Moses, but they don't know what they are talking about, even though they speak so confidently.

I have a good friend of mine and when it comes to work, she is on the ball; she naturally is a helper. When she disclosed that she wanted to start a business but had so much anxiety and fear towards her plans, I was shocked. This scripture stuck to me as it can be scary to start something new but you must know as a believer, fear is not from God. Those plans, those ideas, why wouldn't they manifest once you keep God in the Centre? Constantly remind yourself that fear doesn't come from God.

Stand boldly and leap into the things that you have been fearful to do. For when God is with you, no one can stand against.

ISAIAH 14:27

*The L*ORD *of Heaven's Armies has spoken—*
who can change his plans?
When his hand is raised,
who can stop him?"

Reeling into something new can be easy for some and hard for many. The talk of making changes, plans and the common sentence we often hear at the beginning of a year;

"This year will be better than the last."

Indeed, that is true but you must connect yourself to God's word and believe that whatever God has planned for you, nothing can stop it. The common doubt in your mind may overshadow what God has in-store for you. Your past, your family, your friends; nothing can stop you from being Great.

Be bold, stay connected to the word and wait and see the good things that will unfold in your life.

PROVERBS 24:3

A house is built by wisdom
and becomes strong through good sense.

Wisdom. Something that most people seem to leave behind but it is one of the keys to prosperity.

When you plan in life it is imperative that wisdom must be used. You build things through wisdom and when you have wisdom, you will be rich in so many ways. Do not put your trust in human beings but believe and seek God for counsel.

May everything you build be built by the spirit of wisdom and may the spirit of wisdom bring you what you have been praying for. By understanding, you will be established.

LUKE 6:12-13

¹² One day soon afterward Jesus went up on a mountain to pray, and he prayed to God all night. ¹³ At daybreak he called together all his disciples and chose twelve of them to be apostles.

Let us declare that this year be the year of 'good things.' You need to make important, life changing decisions but you leave God out. Pray about the decision you are going to make. As you read in the scripture, Jesus prayed all night to God and by morning he made his decision. Even Jesus prayed, who are you not to pray about the decisions you will make.

One day I will elaborate the importance of prayer in decision making, but today my prayer is that you will be strong-willed and stand in prayer.

May you spend time in God's presence so that he may grant you your answer as you pray.

2 CORINTHIANS 5:7

For we live by faith, not by sight.

My favourite scripture of all time. A scripture that has helped me to deal with things in the past and a scripture that helps me to progress. To be able to do as it says is easier said than done, especially when a situation arises. If we allow everything negative we hear to channel us, then we are not exercising our faith.

No matter what the situation, in times of need may we look to our father to help restore us and to be able to look forward and face any situation that arises.

Let our faith be unshakeable.

MATTHEW 6:6

But when you pray, go away by yourself, shut the door behind you, and pray to your Father in private. Then your Father, who sees everything, will reward you.

There are many types of prayer, for example when you pray together as a church or in a group. We must reach a point in our lives where we feel comfortable enough to pray as an individual, so that we can engage in a one to one prayer with God. Having that personal prayer with the father connects us to him personally. Most will say, I don't know how to start, which is quite common but I encourage you to talk to God.

Lay your burdens before him, ask him to see your heart and most importantly ask him for forgiveness. Talk to him and have that connection; trust me your personal time with God counts.

SCRIPTURES FOR UPLIFTMENT AND ADVICE.

"When you go through deep waters, I will be with you. When you go through rivers of difficulty, you will not drown. When you walk through the fire of oppression, you will not be burned up; the flames will not consume you."
- Isaiah 43:2

PHILIPPIANS 4:6

Don't worry about anything; instead, pray about
everything. Tell God what you need and thank him for
all he has done.

There have been times when God has used some of my family and friends to speak this scripture into my life. In this moment, I want to share this with you. A situation may be happening in your life where you allow your heart to be full and continue to think and evaluate the situation. You may have a heart's desire to get married, have a child or for something to do with your career or family. Speak to God and let him know your request.

As one of my aunties used this line to encourage me, I will also use the same to encourage you; If God can do it for me, then he definitely can do it for you.

2 CORINTHIANS 9:8

And God will generously provide all you need. Then you will always have everything you need, and plenty left over to share with others.

Don't keep stressing about that interview you have. Stop overthinking about the business you have just started. Stop listening to people's ungodly advice. My God is unshakable and unstoppable. He is the only God that can bless you beyond your wildest dreams. I dare you to trust in him.

So, stop fretting. You shall do well for my God says so.

PROVERBS 27:17

As iron sharpens iron, so a friend sharpens a friend.

We are living in a time where friendships seem to diffuse over small things. The essence of friendship is no longer valued. Remember, when iron sharpens iron it becomes sharper and more effective. So, when two people come together and form a friendship they become stronger together. A good friend doesn't always have to agree with what you say, a good friend is somebody who lovingly challenges you to be a better person.

Ask yourself, do you have that friend?

PROVERBS 18:21

The tongue can bring death or life;
those who love to talk will reap the consequences.

You eat the fruit of what you speak. Speak results into existence, don't wait for it to happen. The power of the tongue is REAL. Speak life into yourself and situations. Simple sentences such as "I am broke", should not come out of your mouth unless you want to own that sentence and eventually become it. Walk boldly and confidently and say;

"I am wealthy!"

"I am healthy!"

"I am blessed!"

As you profess it with your tongue it shall come to pass.

JEREMIAH 29:11

For I know the plans I have for you," says the Lord. *"They are plans for good and not for disaster, to give you a future and a hope.*

As you grow, you realise that the plans you had for your life haven't exactly matched up to the ones you had when you were younger. At times, you fell into the traps you wish you didn't encounter and you have had to start over again. The plan God has for your life will NOT bring you to shame. God has a call on your life. You may have gone around the world to avoid him but God has a way of bringing you back.

You may feel like you have lost everything but I tell you it's just the beginning, the beginning of God calling you to walk in your future, the future where you will prosper.

ISAIAH 57:13

Let's see if your idols can save you
when you cry to them for help.
Why, a puff of wind can knock them down!
If you just breathe on them, they fall over!
But whoever trusts in me will inherit the land
and possess my holy mountain.

False Idols.

When you think of those two words you automatically think about the Ten Commandments and the commandment which mentions false idols. Friends and materialistic things are also classed as false idols and sometimes if you are not careful, you end up worshipping them more than God himself.

Where does it say that if a friend doesn't talk to someone you must follow? Is that your friend or your God?

This can be a modern typical example of how others allow themselves to idolise friends. Let us be wise and follow God's word to get a deeper understanding. When all those idols are gone and blown away it is only God that we then end up crying to.

A prayer I pray constantly is more of God and less of myself.

Subconsciously we follow things and people without the knowledge and concept of it. Then when things go wrong, we question it; why does it always have to come to that?

I pray for myself and everyone reading this that we may receive wisdom and know you alone are God – not friends, objects or even family. May we find refuge in you O' Lord and know that greater things will be ahead of us.

LUKE 6:38

Give, and you will receive. Your gift will return to you in full—pressed down, shaken together to make room for more, running over, and poured into your lap. The amount you give will determine the amount you get back.

Usually festive seasons are the only time where people give gifts to others or give donations to charities, homeless people, women's refuge etc.

We should learn how to give always – and not just because of the season.

Be a cheerful giver and let it be a lifestyle. I guarantee you the blessings that follow will be the miracles you were never expecting.

JEREMIAH 4:3

Plow up the hard ground of your hearts!
Do not waste your good seed among thorns.

Going forward, bare fruits from the things around you. Whatever you left behind that was barren, whether it was that business idea or even a mortgage application; pick it up and break your fallow grounds. Do not waste time on things that are not working as those are the thorns that are not worth sowing into.

Invest your labour into things that will make you great. Don't look back, look forward and whatever you sow your time into will work.

LUKE 17:4

Even if that person wrongs you seven times a day and each time turns again and asks forgiveness, you must forgive.

Out of all the scriptures I have quoted, this one by far has been the most difficult to acknowledge. This is not because I don't forgive at all, it just brought me to a strange place, which most of you may identify with. I saw an old acquaintance the other day and I had mixed feelings. The person was trying to get my attention – whether it was for good intentions or not I didn't know. In that moment I had to ask myself if I had truly forgiven that person, or had I just purely chosen to forget? I know I am not alone when I write this and it is a prayer I desire for myself as well as you; that God will continue to soften our hearts, and grant us peace and the willingness to forgive easily.

1 SAMUEL 16: 13

So as David stood there among his brothers, Samuel took the flask of olive oil he had brought and anointed David with the oil. And the Spirit of the LORD came powerfully upon David from that day on. Then Samuel returned to Ramah.

Samuel came to David's Father Jesse and tells him that the Lord instructed him that one of his sons would be a king. When all seven sons were presented, none were chosen. The Lord said to Samuel to ask Jesse if he had anymore sons and Jesse replied yes, that there was one more, the youngest, who was out in the field with the sheep. A couple of verses earlier, Samuel had thought the first son Eliab was to be anointed because of his appearance but the Lord showed Samuel it is not the way someone looks, but it is their heart (I encourage you to read the whole chapter).

In life, people are chosen for certain blessings and are favoured not because of what they look like but because of their heart. Just as David stood among his brothers and was anointed by Samuel, may you receive the same blessings. Anyone who doubted you and your heart for God, may that stand in awe when it is your appointed time to rise into blessing.

JOHN 15:7

But if you remain in me and my words remain in you, you may ask for anything you want, and it will be granted!

It is all good when you know Christ for yourself and you're on your own personal journey with him but — and there is a but — when you read the scriptures within the bible, do you stand on a verse or verses for your own situation?

Most people do, and some don't know how to, which is ok. Today you may learn something new or you may remember that it has been said to you before.

Decide what you want from God and find a scripture or scriptures that match it and learn to keep them in your heart. Be ready to use it against the demons who will be little against it and remember to use it daily, for it will come to pass.

Secure the word in your heart and it will be your portion.

GALATIANS 6:7

Do not be deceived: God cannot be mocked. A man reaps what he sows.

Most of us would not be where we are, had it not been for some prayers invested on us by our parents and grandparents. They sowed in us so that we may reap the rewards later in life. As a Christian, you work and devote your energy to the work of God but sometimes you get to a point of standstill and people ask you where your God is. The good news is that God is a faithful rewarder of those that diligently do his work.

Whatever you find yourself doing, do it with all your might and strength and you will reap abundantly. As a student, when you study hard you get rewarded with good grades. It is a key principle in life that whatsoever a man sows, so shall he reap.

Sow good and you will harvest good when the time comes. Let this principle guide you in all your life endeavours.

PROVERBS 18:24

There are "friends" who destroy each other,
but a real friend sticks closer than a brother.

When you read this scripture it looks straightforward but unfortunately, most of us haven't been able to align ourselves with it.

At times, we assume that the person we have known the longest will be the one that will stick by us but a lot of the time that is not the case. If a friend is ready to bare all their problems to you for you to support them, but in your times of need they are scarce; was it friendship or was it convenience? I have learnt that the greatest gift that a friend can do is to pray and intercede for me, amongst supporting me whether in good or bad times. This is Priceless.

Prayer can change a situation and if that person is willing to stand in the gap for you, that is a real friend. My advice would be to check your surroundings and analyse your circle well. God will lead you to that person who will stick by you, pray for you and be there to support you, but most importantly learn how to be that example of a friend, so that the love may flow.

1 PETER 5:9

Stand firm against him and be strong in your faith.
Remember that your family of believers[a] all over the
world is going through the same kind of suffering
you are.

We must always stay alert and be aware that even if things are going well at a stage, the devil is always ready to catch us slipping when we least expect it. Keep your guard up. There are many ways to resist the devil, but firstly you must stand strong in your faith and know that you are not the only one that is going through certain hurdles in life, other believers are as well.

May you stand strong in prayer. Do not be delusional. Equip yourself with the word of God, for the hurdle you are going through will not last for long.

MATTHEW 7:24

Anyone who listens to my teaching and follows it is wise,
like a person who builds a house on solid rock.

It is imperative for us to allow ourselves to listen to God. Whenever I hear someone close to me say;

"My friend said I should do this" or "My friend said I should do that."

My initial reaction is what has God said? On several occasions, many of us find ourselves wanting to hear from what people around us have to say. If we used the same energy we use when listening to other people and allow ourselves to hear from God instead, most of us wouldn't be in some of the predicaments we may find ourselves in today.

Learn to listen and wait on God. Be obedient and put it into practice. It is not easy but I promise you, the favour attached to it is indescribable. Be wise.

1 TIMOTHY 2:2

Pray this way for kings and all who are in authority so that we can live peaceful and quiet lives marked by godliness and dignity.

This scripture screamed at me one Sunday during a sermon and it just so happened that my sister and I were talking about the local elections and voicing our opinions on it, which were not great. Hearing this scripture basically shaped my thoughts and made me realise that I may not like who is in authority, but as a believer it is not about liking or disliking the government; it is about praying for them.

Pray that God may change their hearts and that peace be attached to any decisions they make. Instead of us disliking the government, let's pray for them.

It's only God that can change the heart of a person. Be Wise.

2 CHRONICLES 15:7

*But as for you, be strong and courageous, for your work
will be rewarded.*

This scripture literally jumped up at me and I literally read it, bowed my head and said thank you Lord. Starting something is never easy and can have its ups and downs like everything else. I want to use this scripture to encourage you. When I started walking in my purpose and set up my ministry 'Ladies in Waiting', trials and tribulations came at me like no man's business. However, I cannot stop praising God for how far it has come in such a short space of time.

Please don't give up. Trials will always come, trust me I could write a book on it. Hold on to that business venture or job you're working so hard at, favour will be your portion.

Always keep God involved and stand firm. Be strong, for all shall be well. I know you can do it.

PSALM 139:14

Thank you for making me so wonderfully complex!
Your workmanship is marvellous—how well I know it

People around me have had their characters threatened or compromised, and it has allowed them to question themselves and the people around them. I remember saying to someone that enough is enough; don't allow someone to keep disrespecting you to the point that you will end up feeling low about it. I had to remind them that they were fearfully and wonderfully made and that unfortunately the person they are having trials with has forgotten. The main thing is that you must never forget it.

No matter what adversity you find yourself, remember your God is greater and his works are wonderful. Don't allow anyone to put you down. Why? Because you are fearfully and wonderfully made. Praise him.

PROVERBS 28:20

The trustworthy person will get a rich reward,
but a person who wants quick riches will get into
trouble

Faithfulness. Having faithfulness is being able to be patient with the process. The process with anything that is happening within your life. Remaining faithful even if challenges are amounting. Many situations in life will test your faithfulness, I can adhere to that one. The scripture says a faithful person will richly be blessed, I receive that declaration for all of us.

We must work on our faithfulness, we must stay committed to the work of God and we must learn to stay loyal. Some may not know but faithfulness and loyalty goes hand in hand and I pray that God will help us increase our loyalty, so we can be blessed to help others

ROMANS 1:12

*When we get together, I want to encourage you in your
faith, but I also want to be encouraged by yours.*

Surround yourself with those who are investing in your life. It is not
about how long you may have known someone or how long they have
known you, all of that does not matter at all.

I have reached a point in my life where, if you do not decide to
carry a certain level of wisdom or you do not help to uplift me, there
is no purpose for me to be around you. I want to be reassured that
once I am in your presence, you would encourage me to remain
consistent in my faith no matter the challenge, as I would do the same.

For anyone who does not have the right people around them to
encourage them through their faith, I pray that God removes them
and surrounds you with helpers of faith that will uplift you, so that
you can also do the same. All shall be well

PSALMS 136:1

_Give thanks to the L_ord_, for he is good!_
His faithful love endures forever.

Oh, give thanks unto the Lord for he is good. This day I want you to give him praise for the things he has done and the things he is about to do. Start off by saying;

> "God, I thank you for where you have brought me from and for where you are going to take me."

Even that alone is massive. It may have been a long road, a tough one too, but in all be thankful as it has allowed you to grow.

For all the projects that you have started and for the projects and ideas that are about to start, learn to thank God for the process and I'm telling you things will move and shift in ways you can't imagine.

- Recommended song: 'Oh, Give Thanks' by Fred Hammond.

PROVERBS 8:35

For whoever finds me finds life
and receives favour from the Lord.

After having various conversations with some of my family and friends, this verse made so much sense. We were created by God to have goals and to press towards them, but fear and doubt which also brings procrastination can leave us doubting a situation.

These thoughts do not allow you to live in confidence and you miss out on the exciting, adventurous life God has for us. Jesus died not only for the forgiveness of our sins but also so that we might enjoy a passionate, fruitful and powerful life in him.

I Pray that God will help you live the adventurous life he has for you and that fear and doubt will not be your portion.

JAMES 3:16

For wherever there is jealousy and selfish ambition, there you will find disorder and evil of every kind.

This scripture stood out as I thought about certain situations that have happened, or are about to happen to people around me.

Sometimes some of us don't know when to come out of toxic environments. We will stay until something bad happens and by that time, it happens to be too late. When the devil is ready to bring confusion; jealousy and selfishness will also be there. Whenever someone is trying to look better than others or get the better of others, things fall apart. Most people want what you don't have, so they scheme and kill to get it. Most people are jealous of what others have, but they can't get it so they fight and wage war to take it away from them.

If you constantly find yourself in that situation, I pray that wisdom will find you and that God will remove certain people and obstacles from your way. Let's want what God wants for us. Let's desire him more.

GALATIANS 1:10

Am I now trying to win the approval of human beings, or of God? Or am I trying to please people? If I were still trying to please people, I would not be a servant of Christ.

I had been discussing a situation and this scripture literally jumped at me as I couldn't have put this better myself. I had seen something on social media, an influencer saying that she was afraid to speak about her faith and put it out there, as she felt that she wouldn't get Sponsors. I was shocked but not amazed at all.

Comprising your faith just for common sponsors doesn't show me that you believe in what God can do for you and the promises he has on your life. When will there be a time where people understand that pleasing human beings is a temporary measure, and it will not get you far.

If you find yourself feeling like this at times, I pray for separation of your thoughts so that your faith will not waver. May the blessings of God locate you as you diligently seek him.

ROMANS 12:12

Rejoice in hope, be patient in tribulation, be constant in prayer.

Too many people are frustrated over the things that may have been prophesied to them, or that they expect to happen within a timeline.

People leave churches out of frustration because, often a pastor has prophesied and they expect the prophesy to happen tomorrow. Others have stopped talking to friends and even family members because they have not reached the level they think they should have reached. Frustration is a feeling that can take you away from your destiny. It blind-sight's you to the things that are in front of you and that alone can cause you to think and act differently. It clouds your vision and separates you from the right people.

Do not allow frustration to steal your joy. Whatever is for you will be for you. Stay patient, stay prayed up and allow yourself to hear from God.

POEMS.

"And he has filled him with the Spirit of God, with wisdom, with understanding, with knowledge and with all kinds of skills."

- Exodus 35:31

THE EPITOME OF STRENGTH
MONOLOGUE

~

I started this year with plans, big plans, something to make my
life move forward. I knew deep down they will execute, and
that extra joy will be the centre of my home.
I didn't know, that my plans would be taken away from me,
these plans weren't no small plans, they were big, I thought it
would heal my desire and fulfil me, instead I stood in an empty
place, a place of uncertainty, a place of sorrow, A place that I
did want to be, a place where my enemies would only wish for
me to be and I felt defeated.
Little did I know that through my tears and sweat and the loss
of blood, the uncountable needles that I had to go through, that
hope will knock on my door. I refused to open it as I was tired,
and I didn't want to disappoint myself any longer, so I never
opened the door, instead I picked myself and went to Schiphol
to clear my head and came back with a false smile as I couldn't
bear the journey ahead.
Again the door knocked and this time the knock was hard, so
hard I had to open the door and eventually I gave in to hope,

Hope showed me that as I had gained her, my strength will renew, I just had to build up the courage to talk to him again and I didn't want to as I had hid myself away because I was upset. Yes, I was upset with the Lord, now I wasn't angry, and I couldn't forget where he brought me from, but I was upset, and I didn't want to focus on it.

That faithful day came and I couldn't sleep, I tossed and turned for hours and then within a minute I broke down, I had cried a river and I turned to him and told him how I felt and that the path I'm on is heavy, I need help and there his word came;

"But those who wait on the Lord Shall renew their strength; They shall mount up with wings like eagles, They shall run and not be weary, They shall walk and not faint."

I learnt, and I'm still learning to wait on my Lord. I'm renewing my strength daily and I know I am the EPITOME OF STRENGTH and you can be also.

MY PETITION

How I have waited, How I have been patient.
I asked you for him and Lord you heard my prayer.
Uncountable cries of outbursts I have had O' Lord
Continuous times of pressure, continuous times of affliction.
When there seemed be no more hope, when I thought joy had
left my soul,
I went on my knees and gave everything within myself to reach
out to you.
You answered my prayer, you remembered me Lord, when I
didn't even remember myself.
For this child I prayed, and the Lord granted my petition that I
made to him
I will be forever grateful, for I know you never forsake me.

Inspired by **1 Samuel 1:27**

THE LORD IS MY SHEPHERD

Surely goodness & mercy shall follow me all the days of my life.
Day by day the turnaround of things looks so distant from me.
Lord I want to be still, I want my soul restored, they see me, and they
laugh, they talk behind my back, but smile in my face.
I know one day surely one day you will present me in front of them,
and they will see the anointing you have placed on me.
Lord I will dwell in the house of the Lord for I know that you are
with me.
The valley of the shadow of death I may walk but I won't fear no evil
for I trust and know you walk with me.
Surely goodness & mercy shall follow me all the days of my life.

Inspired by **Psalm 23**

POEM FOR SINGLES

SINGLENESS

Enjoy this time in your life, they say.
Make sure you do everything before you settle down.
Hearing this makes me roll my eyes, do they know how it feels
to be in this way?
I used to think this all the time, and I never once thought to
myself, are they right.
Weddings, upon weddings, I have encountered, yet I still do not
find my one, every so often I get the nudge, that infamous one,
what do you think of him? or why don't you shine your eye
well well, or when will you marry?
I cannot express the way I feel as it seems they may have forgot
how it felt for them. I mean being single isn't that bad, and I
know when the time is right he or she will come along, who am
I kidding.
I need to find what makes me ecstatic, a drive that keeps me
going, an enjoyment filled within me like no other.
I need to start with myself and know that I may be alone, but I

am not lonely. I am in this season to realise a relationship does not define who I am, but with Christ I am a whole new identity.

I choose to start with myself, I choose to walk in my purpose, I choose to connect with my destiny, after all whoever God connects me with, they must and will align with my destiny.

POEM OF LOVE

LOVE ARRIVES

The key to love is understanding the ability to comprehend not only the spoken word but those unspoken gestures the little things that say so much by themselves. Love arrives and, in its train, comes ecstasies of old memories of pleasure, ancient histories of pain. Yet if we are bold, love strikes away the chains of fear from our souls. When I think back that I thought I knew what love was, it's now I realise that love is standing right here in my face. I was in a tunnel so dark not knowing if the light would be found. But God never slept, he never forsakes me, and patiently watched me grow and bought you as my light that will continue to shine. Together we will be stronger than we could be alone, I know together our love will grow into a bond too strong not to hold. In the centre we shall keep him there, and know that with God in the midst, we can conquer all.

Extracts from **Ohemaa's Wedding Vows**

POEM FOR THE WOMAN FINDING
HER WAY

ANTICIPATION

Your words are so blissful it gives peace to my heart
Yet when we're together it feels like we're apart.
The understanding and principles of our words
Are they often things that go unheard?
The sense of feelings runs away with our thoughts
And we act as if we've never been taught.
The gift of time runs away with our minds
Caught in the trap where feelings can be confined.
Every heartbeat is an explosion of emotions,
To my heart, to my mind? Or straight to my soul….
This is no ordinary explosion; its my life you stole
Taking something incomplete and making it whole.
Your words are forever blissful bringing peace to my heart.

I AM NOT BARREN

Dear Sis,
Wipe your tears, get rid of your fears. Easier said than done
right? You are a woman of principle. Hold your head up high.
You haven't been able to conceive, they may call you barren,
but I know God will allow you to conceive, and you will bear a
child, renew your strength in the Lord, prepare yourself, for
he/she is coming, just as Samson.

**The angel of the Lord appeared to her and said, "You
are barren and childless, but you are going to
become pregnant and give birth to a son. As
conceived, you will also receive that blessing"**
- Judges 13:3-5.

*Inspired by **Judges 13: 3-5 (Samson's mother was barren)***

MY INTENTIONAL JOURNEY

You will begin life with some friends and you may not end up
with them within your journey
Hard to absorb right? That friend who you grew up, that friend
who saw you at your worst, may not be there in the next
season, its hard to swallow, but I'm experiencing it now.
You see life is like a bus journey and you have a destination to
reach. Every friend that comes on that journey may not reach
YOUR destination, but YOU must find your way to get there.
I really wanted her to come, I honestly did. I didn't understand
why she decided to come off that stop, is it because my
decisions were different to hers? Is it because she had
insecurity issues and didn't know her worth and I did. I stood
up when she decided she was going to get off, I tried my best to
keep her on, she pushed me away and didn't want me by her
side, I mean family functions, she didn't invite me anymore, I
watched the photos on social media and sighed. She would
only message me when it was convenient, but I continued to
keep her by my side.
She finally came off and I looked through the window and

stared. I mean maybe one day she may come back on but for now she is gone.

I now know that I must keep focused on my destination and I should not get distracted, as the road is long, and I know I shall get there with or without those I started with.

Inspired by **Philippians 1:6**

CLOSING TESTIMONY

*E*very scripture chosen and interpretation written has been done so from my soul. Some of these scriptures are dearer to me as I turned to them to guide myself through situations that I had been going through and this enabled me to gain a better understanding and meaning of them.

As THERAPEUTIC AS this journey has been for myself, I never imagined how much it would impact so many others – non believers in particular who became intrigued and wanted to know more about God. It was this that kept me writing and pushed me out of my comfort zone, knowing that this book would help myself and so many others.

THE JOURNEY I have embarked on and the journey ahead is bigger than I could ever have imagined. I pray that I continue to be great and guide others on a path to do the same.

- ABIGAIL OHEMAA AFRIYIE

TESTIMONIALS

Morning , well firstly thanks for sending these messages out. God will reward you for your faithfulness and sacrifice.

For me , your messages have either confirmed something God has placed in my heart or an uplift to challenges.
- *Jolene*

"I wanted to thank you for a conversation you had with me a while back about being saved, sex before marriage and dating someone non-Christian. I've given my life to Christ fully and I'm going to be baptised next month.
When you said what you said to me to me I was taken back and was against what you said but now I fully understand, and I thank you for being real with me. I've put off writing this message but I think it is important that I tell you.
Continue your ministries and I pray god continues to bless you and those who come into your presence."
- Chloe

"I feel like it has helped with my faith. Times that I am feeling low it has helped lift up my faith. Three weeks ago I was feeling so down and feeling like I was the only person going through things until I read the devotional message and spoke with Abigail. After speaking to her she encouraged me and reassured me that she had her own problems. That God is planning and working something out, that we just need to trust him."
- Charlotte

ABOUT THE AUTHOR

*A*bigail Ohemaa Afriyie is a loving wife, mentor and confidant. Her 'Ohemaa Speaks' brand and platform allows people from around the globe and of indigenous cultures to come and collaborate through the means of empowerment and showmanship. She also has a women's ministry called Ladies In Waiting and a business called Feed your Faith.

Abigail Ohemaa Afriyie is an advocate of the word and her lifestyle, alongside her significant experiences guide her into giving much needed advice to her audience. She is an inspiration to anyone who crosses her path.